SPACE
MYSTERIES

IS THERE LIFE ON MARS?

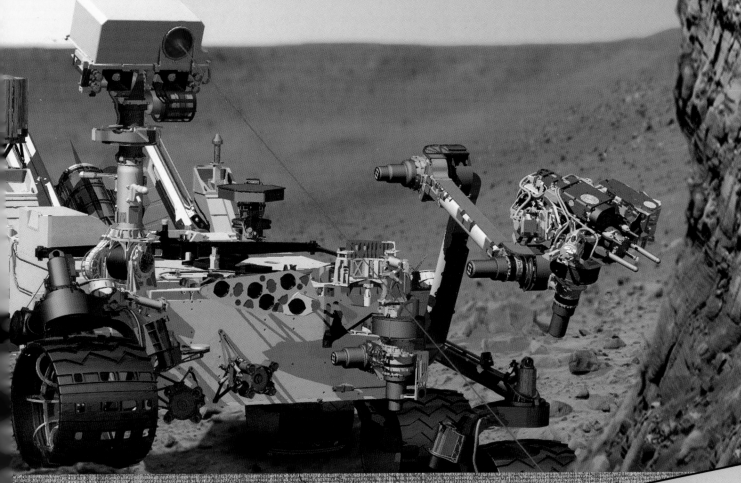

 Gareth Stevens
Publishing

BY MICHAEL PORTMAN

Please visit our website, www.garethstevens.com. For a free color catalog of all our high-quality books, call toll free 1-800-542-2595 or fax 1-877-542-2596.

Library of Congress Cataloging-in-Publication Data

Portman, Michael, 1976-
 Is there life on Mars? / Space Mysteries
     p. cm. — (Space mysteries)
 Includes bibliographical references and index.
 ISBN 978-1-4339-8273-6 (pbk.)
 ISBN 978-1-4339-8274-3 (6-pack)
 ISBN 978-1-4339-8272-9 (library binding)
 1. Mars (Planet)—Juvenile literature. 2. Life on other planets—Juvenile literature. I. Title. II. Series: Space mysteries.
 QB641.P67 2013
 523.43—dc23
                                        2012027588

First Edition

Published in 2013 by
Gareth Stevens Publishing
111 East 14th Street, Suite 349
New York, NY 10003

Copyright © 2013 Gareth Stevens Publishing

Designer: Katelyn E. Reynolds
Editor: Therese Shea

Photo credits: Cover, pp. 1, 29 NASA/JPL–Caltech; cover, pp. 1, 3–32 (background texture) David M. Schrader/Shutterstock.com; pp. 3–32 (fun fact graphic) © iStockphoto.com/spxChrome; p. 5 Digital Vision/Thinkstock.com; p. 7 Aaron Rutten/Shutterstock.com; p. 9 Detlev van Ravenswaay/Picture Press/Getty Images; p. 11 NASA/National Geographic/Getty Images; pp. 13, 17 StockTrek Images/Getty Images; p. 15 InterNetwork Media/Photodisc/Getty Images; p. 16 Steven Hobbs/StockTrek Images/Getty Images; p. 18 NASA/JPL–Caltech/University of Arizona/Texas A&M University; p. 19 NASA/JPL–Caltech/University of Arizona; p. 21 ESA via Getty Images; p. 22 William West/AFP/Getty Images; p. 23 Omikron Omikron/Photo Researchers/Getty Images; p. 25 Encyclopaedia Britannica/Universal Images Group/Getty Images; p. 27 NSSDC/NASA.

Printed in the United States of America

CPSIA compliance information: Batch #CW13GS: For further information contact Gareth Stevens, New York, New York at 1-800-542-2595.

CONTENTS

Words in the glossary appear in **bold** type the first time they are used in the text.

LIFE BEYOND EARTH

Have you ever noticed a bright red star on a clear night? That isn't a star—it's the planet Mars. For centuries, people's imaginations have run wild wondering what Mars is like. Is it like Earth? Are there creatures living on Mars? If so, what are they like? Should we fear them or should they fear us?

Over the years, we've learned a lot about Mars. But the biggest question hasn't been answered yet: Is there life on Mars?

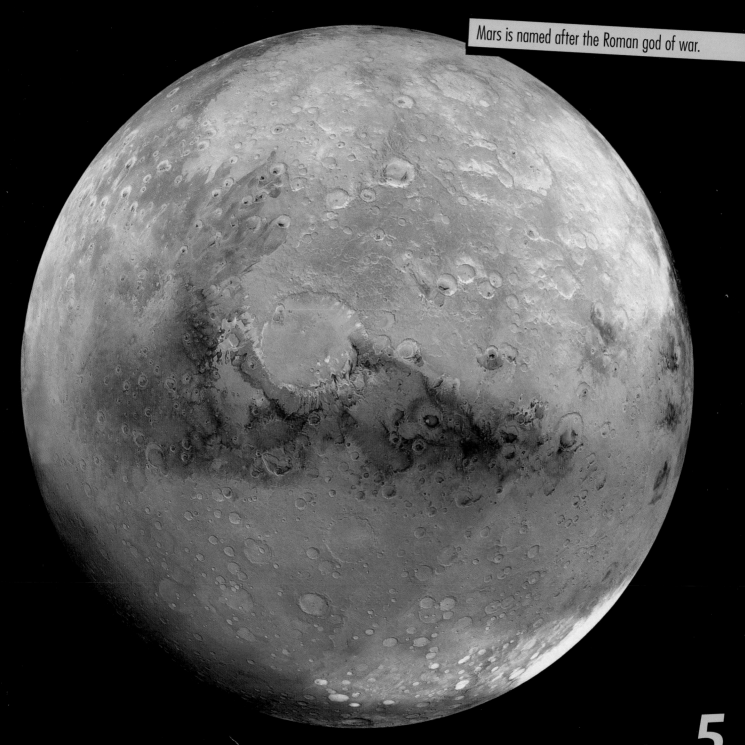

Mars is named after the Roman god of war.

5

MEET THE NEIGHBORS

Mars is the fourth planet from the sun. That makes Mars one of our closest neighbors in the solar system. A solar system is made up of planets, moons, and anything else that circles, or orbits, a star. There are eight planets in our solar system. The four planets closest to the sun are the small rocky planets Mercury, Venus, Earth, and Mars.

The next four planets are Jupiter, Saturn, Uranus, and Neptune. These planets are made of a mix of hydrogen and helium gas.

OUT OF THIS WORLD!

Mars and Jupiter are separated by thousands of asteroids in the "asteroid belt." An asteroid is a piece of rock or metal in space.

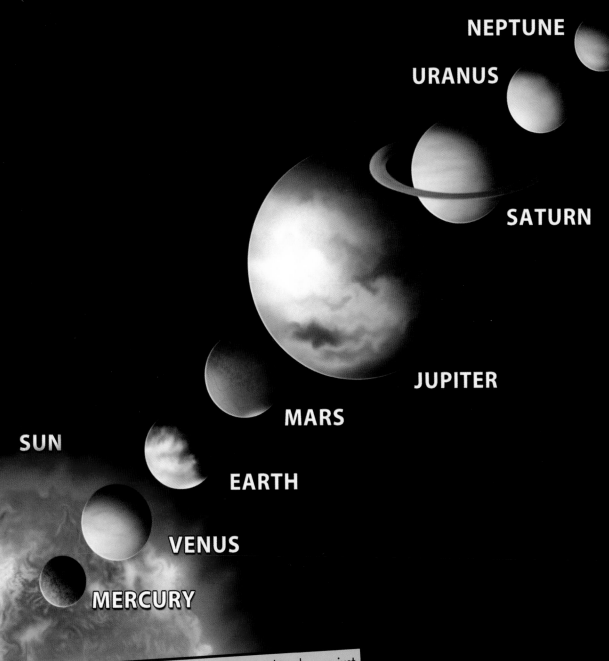

NEPTUNE

URANUS

SATURN

JUPITER

MARS

SUN

EARTH

VENUS

MERCURY

Pluto is a dwarf planet beyond Neptune. Though it orbits the sun just like these planets, it isn't large enough to be considered a planet.

MARTIAN CANALS

When Mars is viewed through a **telescope**, it can look similar to Earth. Many early **astronomers** thought they saw oceans and landmasses on Mars. In the late 1800s, the Italian astronomer Giovanni Schiaparelli drew a map of Mars. His map showed a system of waterways, or channels, that cut across the planet's surface.

A few years later, the American astronomer Percival Lowell announced that the natural channels on Mars were actually canals that had been built to carry water. He thought an **intelligent** form of life had created them.

OUT OF THIS WORLD!

In 1609, the Italian astronomer Galileo became the first person to observe Mars through a telescope.

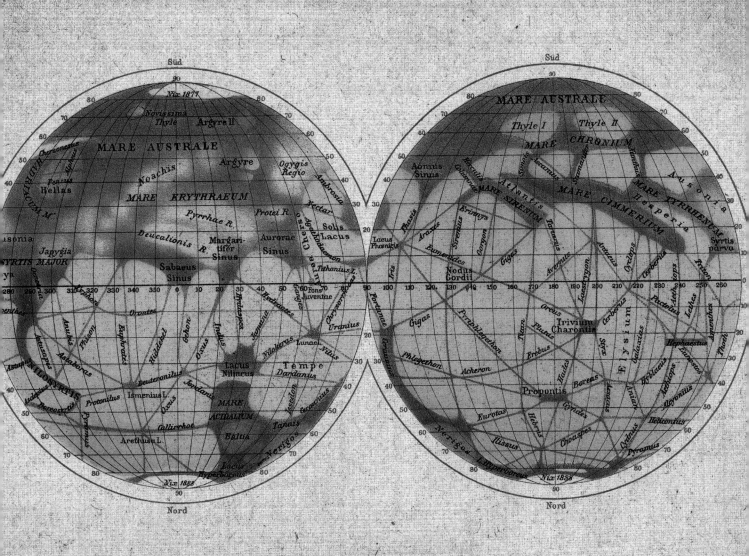

9

SEEING IS BELIEVING

It turned out that Giovanni Schiaparelli, Percival Lowell, and many early astronomers were wrong. There are no canals on Mars. There are no oceans either. Early telescopes simply weren't powerful enough to see what was really on the surface of Mars.

But no one knew what the surface of Mars looked like until many years later. In 1965, the *Mariner 4* spacecraft provided the first close-up photos of Mars. It looked very different from the water-filled planet Lowell had pictured.

OUT OF THIS WORLD!

Huge dust storms can sweep across large parts of Mars for months at a time.

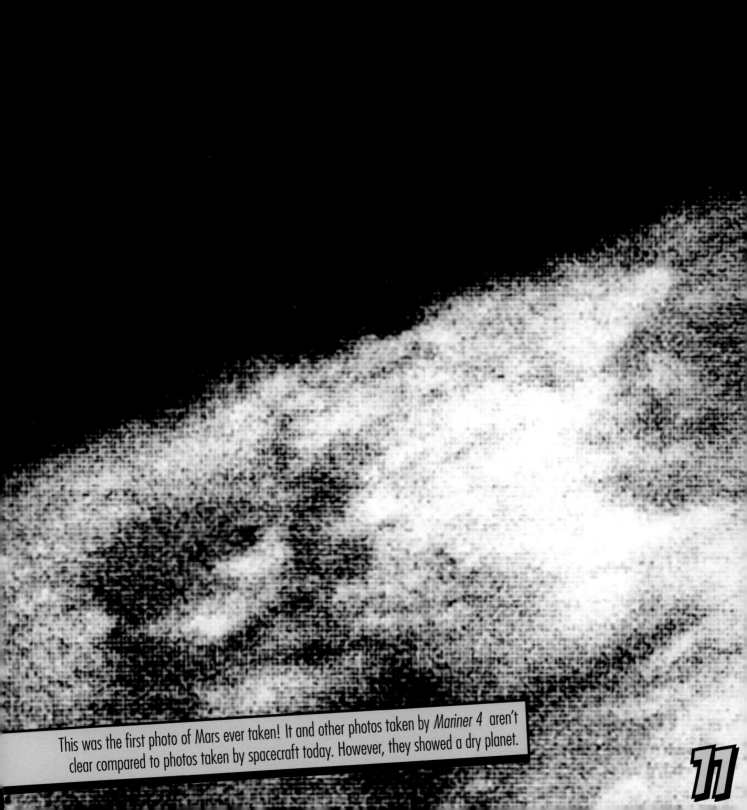

This was the first photo of Mars ever taken! It and other photos taken by *Mariner 4* aren't clear compared to photos taken by spacecraft today. However, they showed a dry planet.

11

THE RIGHT SPOT

Earth sits in just the right spot in our solar system. It's not too close to the sun or too far away. Earth is in the perfect place to support life. Scientists call this spot near the sun the habitable zone. "Habitable" means suitable for life. Life as we know it can only exist inside the habitable zone.

In our solar system, Mars sits on the outer edge of the habitable zone. That's why scientists have spent so much time looking for life there.

OUT OF THIS WORLD!

Mercury and Venus are too close to the sun. **Temperatures** are too hot for life to exist on those planets.

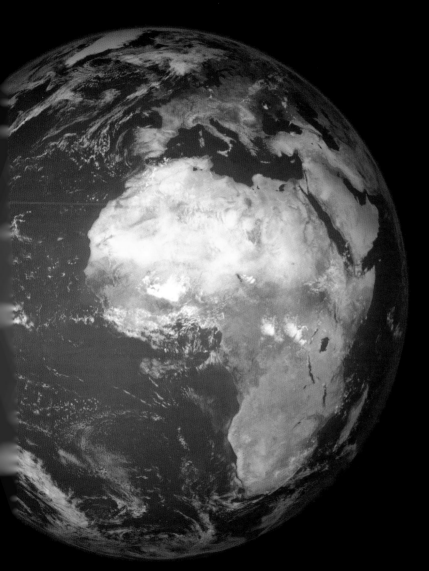

Mars is about half the size of Earth.

13

THE RED PLANET

Mars is the most Earthlike planet in our solar system. Even so, Mars wouldn't seem like home to us! It's cold and dry. It's home to many volcanoes, although none are active. The entire surface is covered with rocks, boulders, and powdery soil.

The soil on Mars contains large amounts of iron. As on Earth, iron turns to rust when it mixes with oxygen. Because rust is reddish in color, Mars is often called "the red planet."

OUT OF THIS WORLD!

The largest mountain in the solar system is on Mars, the volcano Olympus Mons. It's over 16 miles (25 km) tall. That's three times as tall as the highest point on Earth, Mount Everest!

This photo of Mars looks like it could have been taken on Earth.
However, notice there are no plants or other signs of life.

THE AIR UP THERE

The layer of gases that surrounds Earth is called the atmosphere. On Earth, our atmosphere is made mostly of a mix of nitrogen and oxygen. We breathe in these gases. We breathe out another mix of gases that includes carbon dioxide.

Mars has a layer of gases surrounding it, too. But Mars's atmosphere is made mostly of carbon dioxide. There's very little oxygen. The amount of carbon dioxide on Mars would be poisonous to us if we breathed it in.

Gale Crater on Mars

Some of the carbon dioxide on Mars is frozen. Frozen carbon dioxide is called dry ice.

17

THE BIG CHILL

Earth's thick atmosphere also keeps our planet warm. It works like a blanket and traps heat. The atmosphere on Mars is very thin and doesn't do a good job of keeping heat from escaping. Some parts of Mars can get as cold as –199°F (–128°C). That's colder than anywhere on Earth!

Scientists think that Mars once had a thick atmosphere that kept the planet warm. Somehow, the atmosphere thinned out, changing the planet forever.

carbon dioxide frost on the surface of Mars

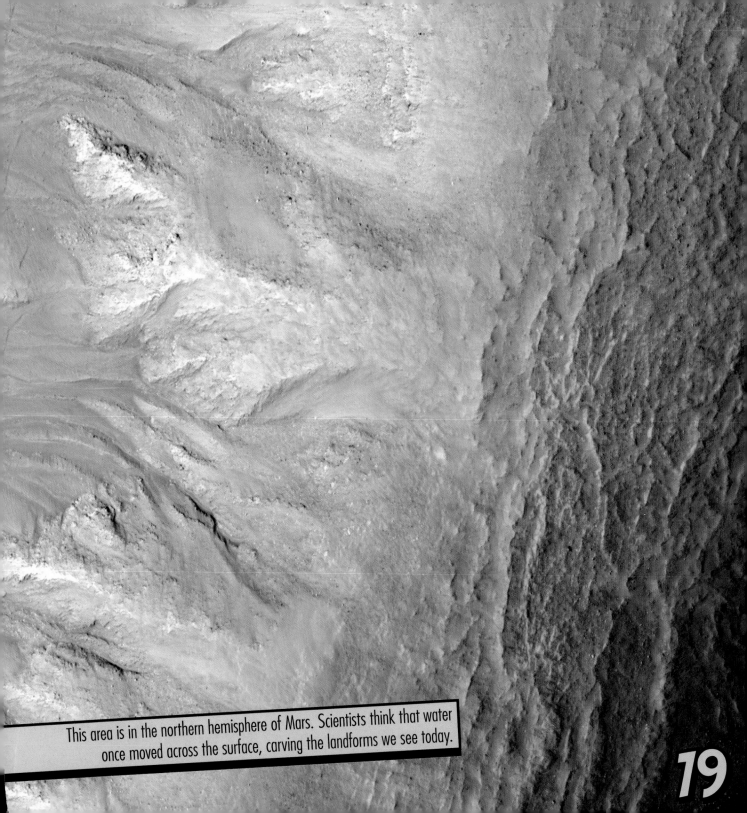

This area is in the northern hemisphere of Mars. Scientists think that water once moved across the surface, carving the landforms we see today.

19

WATER AND ICE

Life on Earth is dependent on liquid water. Scientists think that life on other planets would also require water. Liquid water allows living things to take in **nutrients**. The water on Mars is frozen. Mars has thick layers of ice at its north and south poles called polar ice caps. There's also ice buried under the soil.

Scientists think that Mars once had flowing water and not just ice. That means it's possible that Mars once had life as well.

OUT OF THIS WORLD!

Recent pictures from Mars show streaks in the soil. However, many scientists believe the streaks were made by sliding sand and not by flowing water.

Some scientists think that water once flowed over these giant cliffs on Mars.

21

LITTLE GREEN MEN

Martians—beings that come from Mars—have been a popular subject of stories for many years. Martians were often imagined as evil beings who wanted to attack our planet. Real life is much different. Instead of Martians **invading** Earth, we've been the ones invading Mars!

Since the 1960s, dozens of spacecraft have been sent to Mars. So far, they've shown us no proof that a **civilization** ever existed on Mars. If there was life on Mars, scientists think it would have been tiny organisms similar to **bacteria**.

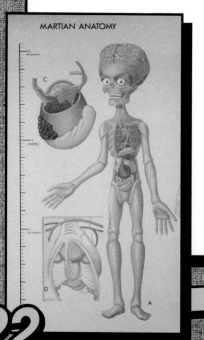

MARTIAN ANATOMY

an artist's idea of a Martian

Today, there are several ongoing **missions** on and around Mars.
Spacecraft today are much more advanced than those of the 1960s.

23

ANCIENT FOSSILS?

In 1996, a group of scientists announced that they had discovered proof of bacteria inside a **meteorite** that fell to Earth from Mars. When they examined the meteorite, the scientists found what looked like the **fossils** of tiny organisms. Scientists now believe that the Mars meteorite doesn't contain fossils. Instead, they think that heat from a volcano on Mars created the shapes inside the meteorite.

Some scientists study unusual forms of life on Earth to discover what things might be able to live in the extreme conditions on Mars.

OUT OF THIS WORLD!

Scientists found bacteria buried under thick ice here on Earth. After the ice melted around it, the bacteria came back to life! Could something similar exist on Mars?

Over the years, several meteorites from Mars were studied for proof of bacteria. None has been found.

MARS PROBES

Most of what we know about Mars comes from the **data** collected by spacecraft. The United States, Russia, and Europe have all sent unmanned spacecraft called probes to Mars. Some probes orbit Mars while others travel on its surface.

In 1976, the *Viking 1* and *Viking 2* landing craft touched down on Mars. They were the first NASA (National Aeronautics and Space Administration) probes to land on Mars. Their mission was to take pictures and search for signs of life. *Viking 2* shut down in 1980, while *Viking 1* operated until 1982.

OUT OF THIS WORLD!

Mars probes use radio waves to send data back to Earth. It takes radio waves several minutes to travel from Mars to Earth.

26

This photo shows part of the *Viking 2* landing craft on the surface of Mars in 1977.

THE SEARCH CONTINUES

In 2004, the **rovers** *Spirit* and *Opportunity* began exploring the surface of Mars. In 2008, NASA's *Phoenix* spent 5 months studying the soil. The most recent NASA Mars mission is the Mars rover *Curiosity*. Sent out in 2011, *Curiosity* is the largest Mars probe yet. It has a drill, laser, cameras, and sensors to help it study rocks and soil.

Some people believe that the best chance of finding proof of life is to send people to Mars. NASA is hoping to send a manned mission to Mars in 2033.

OUT OF THIS WORLD!

Some scientists think Mars could be changed into a habitable planet, a process called terraforming.

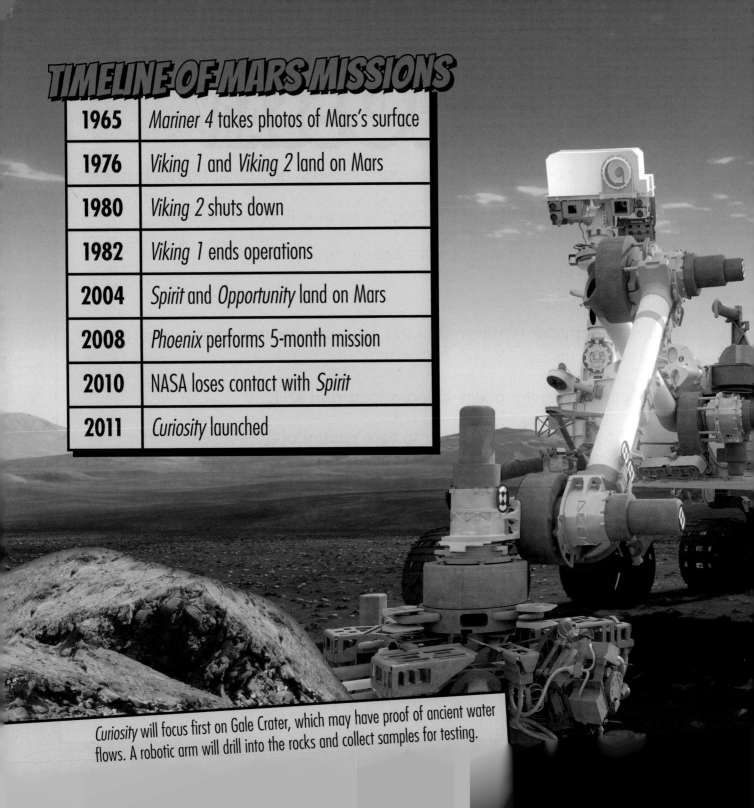

TIMELINE OF MARS MISSIONS

1965	*Mariner 4* takes photos of Mars's surface
1976	*Viking 1* and *Viking 2* land on Mars
1980	*Viking 2* shuts down
1982	*Viking 1* ends operations
2004	*Spirit* and *Opportunity* land on Mars
2008	*Phoenix* performs 5-month mission
2010	NASA loses contact with *Spirit*
2011	*Curiosity* launched

Curiosity will focus first on Gale Crater, which may have proof of ancient water flows. A robotic arm will drill into the rocks and collect samples for testing.

GLOSSARY

astronomer: a person who studies stars, planets, and other heavenly bodies

bacteria: tiny creatures that can only be seen with a microscope

civilization: organized society with written records and laws

data: facts and figures

fossil: the marks or remains of plants and animals that formed over thousands or millions of years

intelligent: having the ability to learn facts and skills

invade: to enter a place in order to take control of it

meteorite: a space rock that has reached Earth's surface

mission: a task or job a group must perform

nutrient: something a living thing needs to grow and stay alive

rover: a small wheeled machine used to explore the surface of a moon or planet

telescope: a tool that makes faraway objects look bigger and closer

temperature: how hot or cold something is

FOR MORE INFORMATION

BOOKS

Carson, Mary Kay. *Far-Out Guide to Mars*. Berkeley Heights, NJ: Enslow Publishers, 2011.

Siy, Alexandra. *Cars on Mars: Roving the Red Planet*. Watertown, MA: Charlesbridge, 2009.

WEBSITES

How Terraforming Mars Will Work
science.howstuffworks.com/terraforming2.htm
Read about the different ways some people think Mars could be made habitable for people.

Life Beyond Earth: Mars
www.pbs.org/lifebeyondearth/alone/mars.html
Find out many cool facts about the red planet.

Solar System Exploration: Mars
solarsystem.nasa.gov/kids/mars_kids.cfm
Learn about Mars on NASA's website.

INDEX